You Are There!

Ancient Egypt

1336 BC

Wendy Conklin, M.A., and Blane Conklin, Ph.D.

Consultants

Timothy Rasinski, Ph.D.
Kent State University

Lori Oczkus, M.A.
Literacy Consultant

Publishing Credits

Rachelle Cracchiolo, M.S.Ed., *Publisher*
Conni Medina, M.A.Ed., *Managing Editor*
Dona Herweck Rice, *Series Developer*
Emily R. Smith, M.A.Ed., *Content Director*
Stephanie Bernard and Seth Rogers, *Editors*
Robin Erickson, *Multimedia Designer*

The TIME logo is a registered trademark of TIME Inc. Used under license.

Image Credits: Cover, p.1 Images of Africa Photobank / Alamy;
p.5 DEA / A. DAGLI ORTI / Getty Images; p.13 Mary Evans Picture
Library / Alamy; p.15 Illustration by Travis Hanson; p.20 (left) Alisdair
Macdonald/REX/Newscom, (right) Sandro Vannini/Corbis; p.22
National Geographic Creative / Alamy; p.25 De Agostini / G. Lovera /
Getty Images; all other images from iStock and/or Shutterstock.

Library of Congress Cataloging-in-Publication Data

Names: Conklin, Wendy, author. | Conklin, Blane, author.
Title: You are there! Ancient Egypt 1336 BC / Wendy Conklin and Blane
  Conklin.
Description: Huntington Beach, CA : Teacher Created Materials, 2016. |
  Includes index. | Includes bibliographical references.
Identifiers: LCCN 2016012333 (print) | LCCN 2016014195 (ebook) | ISBN
  9781493836024 (pbk.) | ISBN 9781480757066 (eBook)
Subjects: LCSH: Egypt--Civilization--To 332 B.C.--Juvenile literature. |
  Tutankhamen, King of Egypt--Juvenile literature. |
  Egypt--History--Eighteenth dynasty, ca. 1570-1320 B.C.--Juvenile
  literature. | Pharaohs--Juvenile literature. | Egypt--Religion--Juvenile
  literature.
Classification: LCC DT61 .C556 2017 (print) | LCC DT61 (ebook) | DDC
  932/.014--dc23
LC record available at http://lccn.loc.gov/2016012333

Teacher Created Materials

5301 Oceanus Drive
Huntington Beach, CA 92649-1030
http://www.tcmpub.com

ISBN 978-1-4938-3602-4

© 2017 Teacher Created Materials, Inc.
Made in China.
Nordica.052016.CA21600902

Table of Contents

Welcome to 1336 BC!

Imagine waking up to find your father has died and you are now the king of Egypt—at only nine years old. It doesn't take long for you to realize that the priests hated your father, Akhenaton, for his extreme religious views. (What was your father thinking when he closed down most of the temples and took away the priests' riches?) Your **advisor**, Ay—who, by the way, was also Akhenaton's right-hand man—is determined to undo your father's hard work. Ay whisks you off to a new home in the city called Memphis. This is where he will rule the ancient land of Egypt through you. And to top off this great news, you will marry your half-sister who is just a few years older than you. Since you are just a kid, you go along with whatever your advisor says. After all, what do you really know about running a country?

Switching Headquarters

Akhenaton had moved the government from Memphis to the new city of Amarna. After Akhenaton died, the advisor Ay moved the government back to its original location in Memphis.

Akhenaton and Queen Nefertiti make an offering

The Sun God

Akhenaton, also known as Aton, declared that the Egyptians should only worship the sun god, Aton. (Notice how they share the same name!) He didn't deny there were other gods. But this action led to closing temples dedicated to other gods. Many priests were suddenly out of jobs and money.

Talking Politics and Religion

There is an unspoken rule that people should never talk about politics or religion. (People have strong opinions about these topics—beware the fights and arguments likely to occur!) But, politics and religion are what make Egypt so interesting. So, let's talk!

Getting into Politics

You might be wondering … who has the power in your kingdom? As king, or **pharaoh**, you have the most power. Your people believe you are half god and can speak directly to the gods—especially about crops—but you turn over many of these duties to the chief priest and other priests. Next to you, your **vizier**, Ay, helps keep an eye on business and what is going on in your kingdom. Ay collects taxes, makes property deals, keeps a running record of your riches, and gives you advice according to what he has learned. Even though you have the right to lead your own army, you rely on Horemheb as your **commander in chief**. Along with Ay, he served your father well, and you have every reason to trust him.

Governors, or **nomarchs**, help maintain order in the smaller counties throughout the kingdom. The nomarchs report to Ay. You trust these rulers because many of them are your relatives. Under the nomarchs are mayors who govern the smallest towns and make sure the rules of society are followed. Village elders serve under the mayors to keep the peace.

The Bottom of the Barrel

At the very bottom of society was the largest group of people, the peasants. They included the men who professionally washed dusty clothes and the fowler who hunted birds eaten for meals. They also included reed cutters, who sold **papyrus** to sandal designers, boat builders, and paper makers. Peasants paid taxes and did jobs that kept Egypt going strong.

STOP! THINK...

- How does the diagram organize jobs from ancient Egypt?
- What is implied about scribes and soldiers in ancient Egypt?
- How can these jobs be compared to jobs today?

pharaoh

vizier

nobles

priests

scribes

soldiers

craftsmen

farmers

slaves

When a Girl Ruled Egypt

Not too long ago, one of your relatives declared herself king … that's right, a *girl* named Hatshepsut. Her father, Thutmose I, spent time training her for the job, since he knew she had potential to be a strong ruler. However, when Thutmose I died, Hatshepsut had to marry her younger half-brother to legitimize his authority as pharaoh because he was only part royal. Her brother was sick most of the time, so Hatshepsut had a lot of say in governing. When the pharaoh died, Hatshepsut's stepson was crowned king—but as he was only a toddler, she served as the **regent** and ruled for him. In no time at all, she took control and declared herself king. She even went as far as to wear a fake beard! She was not the only one to wear a fake beard. All rulers do it, and you will too. Egyptians hate facial hair, but wearing a fake beard is a sign that you, the ruler, identify with the gods.

statue of Hatshepsut

Once Hatshepsut took over, she created **propaganda** to establish her position as king. She had stories carved into the temples that told of her right to rule Egypt; for example, the gods had overseen her divine birth and education. The stories were a great political move on her part, and her leadership was accepted. That's a good thing because during her reign she was responsible for groundbreaking trade agreements with other countries.

The Catfish King

Around 3100 BC, the lower part of Egypt united with the upper part of Egypt. Historians believe the new ruler of this combined Egypt was named Narmer. He is sometimes referred to as the Catfish King because the **hieroglyph** of his name is a picture of a catfish. This began the first dynasty of kings. Other rulers of ancient Egypt include:

Khufu, a fourth dynasty king, was in charge of building the Great Pyramid at Giza.

Pepi II of the sixth dynasty died when he was 100 and was the oldest Egyptian ruler.

Ramses I was a handpicked soldier who ascended to be pharaoh. He only ruled for two years, but there were many more rulers named Ramses after him!

Ramses II is better known as Ramses the Great. He is the most well-known Ramses.

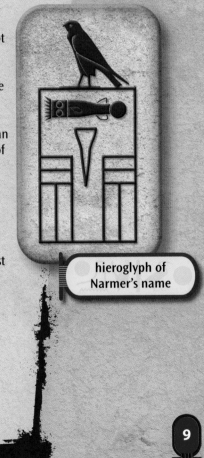

hieroglyph of Narmer's name

Religion in Ancient Egypt

Since your father, Akhenaton, worshipped the sun god Aton, he named you Tutankhaton. (Do you see the resemblance? Your names both end with the sun god's name.) For hundreds of years, the Egyptians had worshipped many gods. These gods had dedicated temples, and priests benefited from these good jobs. No ruler had ever done away with the worship of the gods in Egypt. Your father, Akhenaton, outlawed the worship of any god except Aton. (Not such a great decision on his part!) Now, chisels chip away at your father's images throughout the country. It appears people want to erase the fact that he ever ruled! You've even heard the word *heretic* to describe him. It's clear that many Egyptians are bitter about Akhenaton's reforms during his rule.

You are probably beginning to understand that names are important here in Egypt. Names have power; for example, your name Tutankhaton means the "living image of the sun god." In other words, you are taking on the sun god's identity. Since Narmer's rule, being both a king and a **deity** is a common thing among Egyptian leaders.

Ay suggests that you change your name to Tutankhamun, and you go along with that to keep the peace. It is the least you can do.

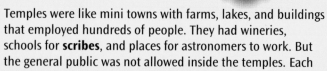

The Temple Towns

Temples were like mini towns with farms, lakes, and buildings that employed hundreds of people. They had wineries, schools for **scribes**, and places for astronomers to work. But the general public was not allowed inside the temples. Each temple served a particular god, not the Egyptians.

Asking for Help

When people needed to make big decisions, they paid visits to the temples to get advice from the gods. There, scribes recorded their requests and handed them to priests. The priests took the requests into the temples, presented them to the gods, and returned with answers.

THINK LINK

◎ Why would Akhenaton's actions upset ancient Egyptians?

◎ Why should King Tutankhamun go along with the changes Ay suggests?

◎ What lessons does this teach about how a ruler should rule his or her people?

Beliefs about the Afterlife

When you die, your spirit will go on to live with the gods in another world. It is important to plan what you will take with you. By burying your possessions, you can be sure to have these items with you in the next life.

Since the body is so important to our society, we will **mummify** it once you die—a step that takes about three months to complete. First, we pull your brain through your nose and discard it. (After all, we believe the brain is not very important.) Next, we remove your liver, lungs, stomach, and intestines and place them into neat little jars that remain in your tomb. However, your heart will stay in your body. The **embalmers** use **natron** to dry out your body and then rub it down with oil. Finally, they wrap it with strips of linen.

During the judgment of the dead, the gods test your goodness by weighing your heart against a feather. If your heart is lighter than the feather, you enter the underworld to live with the god Osiris. The heart is heavy if it is weighed down with sin, and then a monster named Ammit eats you. You will know this monster by its crocodile mouth, wildcat body, and hippopotamus hindquarters. You have little to worry about though; kings typically survive this judgment and go on to live with their preserved bodies in the afterlife.

Surviving the Trip

Before a person could get to his or her **ancestors** in the afterlife, he or she had to go on a long trek through the underworld. The sun god took the deceased on a ferry through the River of Death. The Book of the Dead was written on a papyrus scroll and helped the deceased navigate the underworld through maps, spells, and tips.

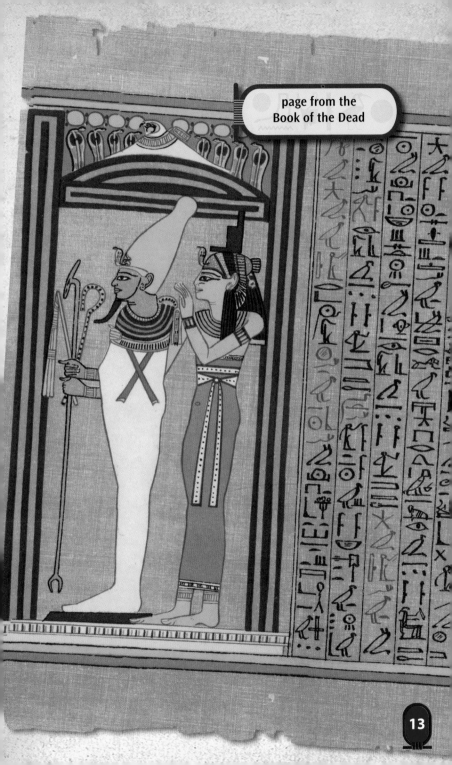

Making a Mummy

Here's how ancient Egyptian embalmers preserved bodies of the dead.

1. They used water or palm oil to wash the dead person's body.

2. Then, they used a long bronze hook to pull out the brain through the nose.

3. They cut out the lungs, liver, stomach, and intestines using the flint knife. The organs were dried in natron and then covered in tree gum. Organs were bandaged and placed in **canopic jars**. Since they believed the dead needed the organs in the afterlife, they preserved them. Four gods, known as the Four Sons of Horus, protected these organs.

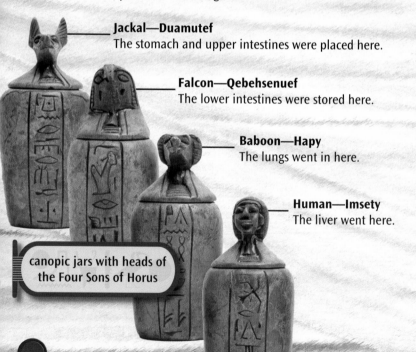

Jackal—Duamutef
The stomach and upper intestines were placed here.

Falcon—Qebehsenuef
The lower intestines were stored here.

Baboon—Hapy
The lungs went in here.

Human—Imsety
The liver went here.

canopic jars with heads of the Four Sons of Horus

4. Next the body was dried out in a natron bath for 40 days.

5. They stuffed the inside of the body with sand, sawdust, or linen.

6. The skin was dry, so to soften it up, they rubbed it with oils and tree gum.

7. A charm was placed over the incision for taking out the organs.

8. They wrapped the body in linen bandages, and placed **amulets** in between some of the linen layers. This took 15 days to complete.

9. A mask of gold was placed over the head and shoulders of the body.

10. They put the body inside a body-shaped wooden coffin, and made sure the coffin was painted with magic spells to keep evil spirits away.

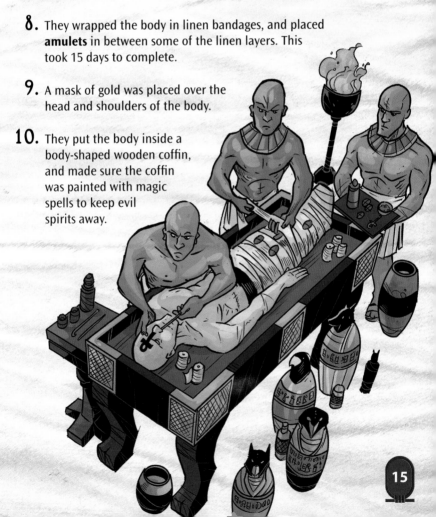

Building a Career

Your life is extraordinary. You spend your days as a young king playing games and hunting wild lions. Though hunting, you are actually training to lead your troops into battle, should you ever go to war. Keep practicing using your slingshot, throwsticks, and bow and arrows! Soon, you will be attending the royal training camp near the pyramids. In the hot desert, you will find plenty of bulls, gazelles, lions, and antelopes to hunt. Take your chariot so you can chase wild ostriches. Your trainer will cry, "Shoot the target! Do not miss!" (That's tough when the chariot and the animal are moving!) As part of this military training, you will also use sticks to wrestle and fight others. After a long day of training, you can relax each night in your **villa** at Giza.

Things can't always be fun, though. It takes real work to be a king. When you get older, you will not only be responsible for protecting Egypt, you will also lead religious festivals. You will keep track of the levels of the Nile River because the water directly affects the harvests. You will also visit your troops throughout the land and entertain foreign visitors.

A Sandal Bearer's Job

The pharaoh had a sandal bearer who held the pharaoh's sandals when he didn't want to wear them. Before putting sandals back on the pharaoh's feet, the sandal bearer is rumored to have kissed the pharaoh's big toe.

Vocations That Serve the King

You are most likely familiar with the jobs that directly affect you, but everyone in Egypt has a job to do. For example, you have fan bearers who carry around ostrich-feather fans and flowers. (That's how the air stays cool and smells better.) Even your magician interprets signs, chants, spells, and views the future so you can make the best decisions.

A Priest's Job

Many priests only worked part time, spending one month in the temples and three months being teachers, doctors, or merchants. Besides making offerings and taking care of the temples, priests presided over ceremonies, funerals, and festivals.

Careers for Smart Folks

If it weren't for scribes, nothing would be written. You see scribes training in the **House of Life**, located in a temple. Most of your people can't read or write, so professional writers are very important for keeping records, writing letters, and recording songs, stories, and poetry. Scribes know more than 800 hieroglyphs. (They should—they've spent eight years studying these symbols.) Some hieroglyphs stand for consonants or combined sounds, while others represent whole words.

Teachers are also priests most of the time. Students learn all the usual subjects such as mathematics, history, reading, and writing. Teachers punish bad behavior with sticks.

Jobs for Strength and Artistry

How would you like to work for eight days straight and then have two days off? If you are a tomb builder, that's your schedule. Since you are king, crews are already building your tomb. Workers begin building a king's tomb the moment he takes the throne. The crew consists of **masons**, scribes, draftsmen, artists, and builders working together to make your tomb stand out among the others. Stonecutters chisel and carve out rooms, and then plasterers line the rooms with plaster. Next, draftsmen and artists paint hieroglyphs and images of the king and the gods.

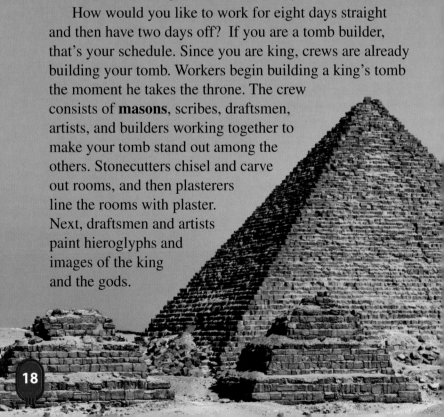

The craftsmen live in tiny villages near the Valley of the Kings, where they enjoy their "pay" (grain, beer, fish, and clothing). Be sure to pay them on time—they **strike** if their pay is late!

The Tallest Building

King Khufu wanted a huge tomb, so he had tomb builders design the Great Pyramid at Giza. It took at least 20,000 workers and 20 years to build the pyramid. And for 4,000 years, it held the record for the tallest building ever. By the time King Tutankhamun ruled, this pyramid was around 1,000 years old!

Tomb Redesign

Long ago, kings were buried under rectangular buildings called **mastabas**. Then, an architect named Imhotep designed a step pyramid for King Djoser. The step pyramid had bricks that grew smaller towards the top of the pyramid.

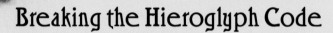

Breaking the Hieroglyph Code

Hieroglyphs are pictures or symbols that represent sounds, objects, or letters. Believe it or not, there was a time when people couldn't read hieroglyphs. Luckily, some Egyptian scribes recorded a text on a stone in three languages: hieroglyphs, Demotic, and Greek. This stone, found near Rosetta, Egypt, unlocked the secrets of hieroglyphs for future generations. Language experts decoded the hieroglyphs because they knew Greek. Today, we call this famous stone the Rosetta Stone.

A **cartouche** is a nameplate attached to a coffin to identify the person inside. Cartouches could be simple or more complex like the cartouche for King Tutankhamun.

Rosetta Stone

Tutankhamun's cartouche

Below are hieroglyphs that make up the sounds of different letters. Use the hieroglyphs to create your own cartouche. Not all sounds are represented with hieroglyphs, so you'll have to do the best you can!

a as in water	*a* as in bat	*b* as in boat	*ch* as in church	*ch* as in loch
d as in dog	*e* as in money	*f* as in foot	*g* as in gone	*h* as in hat
h as in ich	*i* as in pin	*j* as in adjust	*k* as in basket	*l* as in lion
m as in man	*n* as in not	*oo* as in zoo	*p* as in pet	*q* as in queen
r as in right	*s* as in saw	*ss* as in glass	*sh* as in shadow	*t* as in top
u as in glue	*v* as in viper	*w* as in win	*y* as in money	*z* as in zebra

Professions to Help the Sick

If you or other wealthy individuals get sick, you rely on doctors. (The poor people don't have enough money for this!) Doctors use either medicine or magic to cure you. Sometimes, they are reluctant to treat you because if you, the king, die during treatment, they will be blamed.

Local dentists treat everything from toothaches to bad breath. They may drill holes in your jaw to relieve pain. Other times, they drive away evil in your mouth by chanting spells. Since your teeth are really healthy, you don't need a dentist for much.

Pharmacists know how to fill 700 prescriptions! Many of your people suffer from indigestion, so the pharmacist prescribes sugar cakes with crushed hog's tooth. You have a headache? Don't worry. A pharmacist will prescribe **sandalwood**.

Training to Be a Doctor

Information about Egyptian medicine is recorded on a long scroll known as the Ebers Papyrus. Those wanting to be doctors during this time in Egypt studied this scroll.

Trades That Make Us Beautiful

The profession of sandal maker is a job only for men. Made from the papyrus plant, sandals can be customized with colors and gold trim. You own about 93 pairs of them! Some of the soles have pictures of your enemies so you can trample them as you walk.

Barbers are also a big deal. It's hot and lice are a problem, so men and women have barbers shave their heads. The latest fad is for boys to wear their hair very short with long locks of hair on the sides, but they only do this until they turn 12. Barbers work in the streets to fix ponytails and braids for girls.

Because of the shaved heads, wigmakers have booming businesses. On special occasions, the wigs come out. Otherwise, people are happy to go bald. Men, women, and children wear the wigs made from plant fibers and sheep wool. Rich people can afford human hair wigs, while poor people settle for extensions.

Cosmetics for Sale

Pharmacists also made cosmetics like eye kohl, a dark eyeliner worn by both men and women. This not only made them look attractive, it also protected their eyes from the glaring sun.

Living Egyptian Style

Your palace is a far cry from the villas and cottages of your people. But while servants fill your halls, other wealthy homes employ help, too. Beautiful pools, shaded yards, and lush farms surround the villas. Each villa has many rooms around a central hall.

One of your high-ranking nobles is throwing a party, and you show up at his villa. You smell the breads even before entering the villa. A pet monkey grabs a cake off the table. The food includes one of your favorites: duck! The sweet smell of wine fills the air. The meal is served in courses, and then the entertainment begins. You see jugglers throwing objects in the air, dancers swinging their hips, and acrobats flying through the air.

Although you've never visited a poor man's home, you know this type of event could never happen there. You have heard that they live in small cottages with only a few rooms used for sleeping, sitting, and eating. That would be much too small for you!

On any given day, you can see people boxing, playing tug-of-war, and rowing, among other sports. Egyptians are competitive people. Palm-tree branches and leather balls stuffed with papyrus make a fun hockey-like game to watch and play.

Together Forever!

In ancient Egypt, parents, adult male children and their spouses, and grandchildren all lived together. As early teens, young girls prepared for marriage. Boys typically waited until they were 20 years old, since they needed to prove themselves in their jobs first. While most couples chose to stay together until death, divorce in Egypt was easily granted.

Dying Young

Even in the royal family, only one in five children actually reached his or her teen years. Many people died of sickness, such as an infected cut on the leg. To protect their children, parents said spells and prayers over them, and children wore amulets for good luck.

Pharaohs, such as Ramses II, traveled in richly decorated chariots.

Depending on the King!

Needless to say, your people look to you, as king, to be their guiding force. After all, you are a god among them and you speak for the gods. Your job is an important one—to pray for rain so the Nile River floods and soaks the nearby farms, to make sure the sun rises tomorrow, and to keep the gods happy.

Last night in a dream, you saw yourself dead. You call upon your interpreter of dreams at the temple to use his dream book to explain the meaning of that dream. He tells you that this actually means you will have a long life and gives you a spell to recite while you eat fish dipped in beer—something that makes the spell work.

You wonder if your interpreter of dreams is telling you the truth about your future as king. Will you live to old age, or will you die an early death because of an infection or something worse? Your people, both wealthy and poor, hope that someday you will produce an heir to the throne. An heir will ensure your people's security. Is there enough time to make that happen? Only time will tell the **legacy** that your rule will leave behind.

Egypt today is a beautiful mixture of both ancient and modern history.

THINK LINK

◉ In what ways were the pharaohs important to the people of Egypt?

◉ What legacies do people today have from ancient Egyptians?

Inheriting the Throne

The pharaoh, chief wife, and even noblemen inherited their jobs for much of Egyptian history. Tutankhamun's advisors Ay and Horemheb had lofty ideas about ruling Egypt. After the king's death, at age 19, they each had a chance to inherit the throne.

Glossary

advisor—an important person who gives advice to the king

amulets—charms with magical and protective powers

ancestors—relatives who have died

canopic jars—jars used to contain the entrails of embalmed bodies

cartouche (kahr-TOOSH)—nameplate attached to a coffin

commander in chief—the leader of the army

deity—god or goddess

embalmers—people who prepare the dead for burial

hieroglyph—picture/symbol that represents a letter or sound

House of Life—training place for scribes and priests

legacy—something learned from the past

masons—people who carve stones and bricks

mastabas—early Egyptian tombs made from sun-dried mud bricks and stone

mummify—to preserve a body by wrapping it in oils, salts, and linens

natron—a mineral found in dried-up lakes used for embalming

nomarchs (NO-mahrks)—governors in ancient Egypt

papyrus—a reed from a plant that is sliced thin and used as paper

pharaoh—the leader of ancient Egypt; a king

propaganda—information intended to persuade

regent—someone who rules on behalf of the real ruler

sandalwood—a nice smelling wood used in Egyptian medicine to cure headaches

scribes—people whose jobs were to record medical procedures, tax records, and court information

strike—a situation in which all workers stop working to protest poor conditions and force a change

villa—a wealthy home in ancient Egypt with many rooms and a great hall

vizier (vuh-ZIHR)—second in charge to the king of Egypt

Index

Check It Out!

Books

Bingham, Jane. 2009. *How People Lived in Ancient Egypt.* PowerKids Press.

Buller, Laura. 2007. *History Dudes: Ancient Egyptians.* Doring Kindersley Publishing.

Butcher, Kristin. 2009. *Pharaohs and Foot Soldiers: One Hundred Ancient Egyptian Jobs You Might Have Desired or Dreaded.* Annick Press.

Hawass, Zahi. 2005. *Tutankhamun: The Mystery of the Boy King.* National Geographic.

McGraw, Eloise Jarvis. 1986. *The Golden Goblet.* Puffin Books.

Snyder, Zilpha Keatley. 2009. *The Egypt Game.* Atheneum Books for Young Readers.

Videos

PBS. *Secrets of the Dead: Ultimate Tut.*

A&E Home Video. *King Tutankhamun: The Mystery Unsealed.* The History Channel

Website

The British Museum. *Ancient Egypt.* http://www.ancientegypt.co.uk/menu.html

Try It!

Now that you have read about the life of a pharaoh in ancient Egypt, it's your turn to describe what life would be like from another Egyptian perspective. Use the diagram on page 7 to help you choose your role. Decide on the best way to share all these important details of your plan.

- What is your position? What do you do?

- How does your work impact the society as a whole?

- What other people might you interact with daily?

- Do you have a family? What do they do?

- Are you happy where you are, or are you envious of people in different classes from you?

About the Authors

Wendy Conklin has been an educator for nearly 25 years. Much of that time was spent as an author and speaker. Blane Conklin is a systems analyst at the University of Texas. He has a doctorate in Near Eastern Languages and Civilizations from the University of Chicago. Together, they have lived in Jerusalem, Chicago, St. Louis, and currently in Round Rock, Texas. They are happily raising two teenage girls and two middle-age dogs.